BOOK

WRITTEN THRU MICHAEL RAWLEY

ILLUSTRATIONS FROM PAPINEAU

BOOK WRITTEN THRU MICHAEL RAWLEY ILLUSTRATIONS FROM PAPINEAU 1972

Copyright © 1982 Michael Rawley

Published by
PLEASE PRESS LTD.
"publishing good works"

First Edition printing: May, 1985

Made in the U.S.A.

All rights reserved.
For information, write:
    PLEASE PRESS LTD.
    Box 3036
    Flint, Michigan 48502

Library of Congress Catalog Card Number: 85-90338

ISBN: 0-938580-00-0

Book

WRITTEN & DESIGNED
BY
Michael Rawley

includes the original

Papineau

illustrations

DEDICATION

This work is dedicated to
my daughter

Nikita

and

everwho reads this

```
    N
    E
 NEXUS
    U
    S
```

with special thanks to

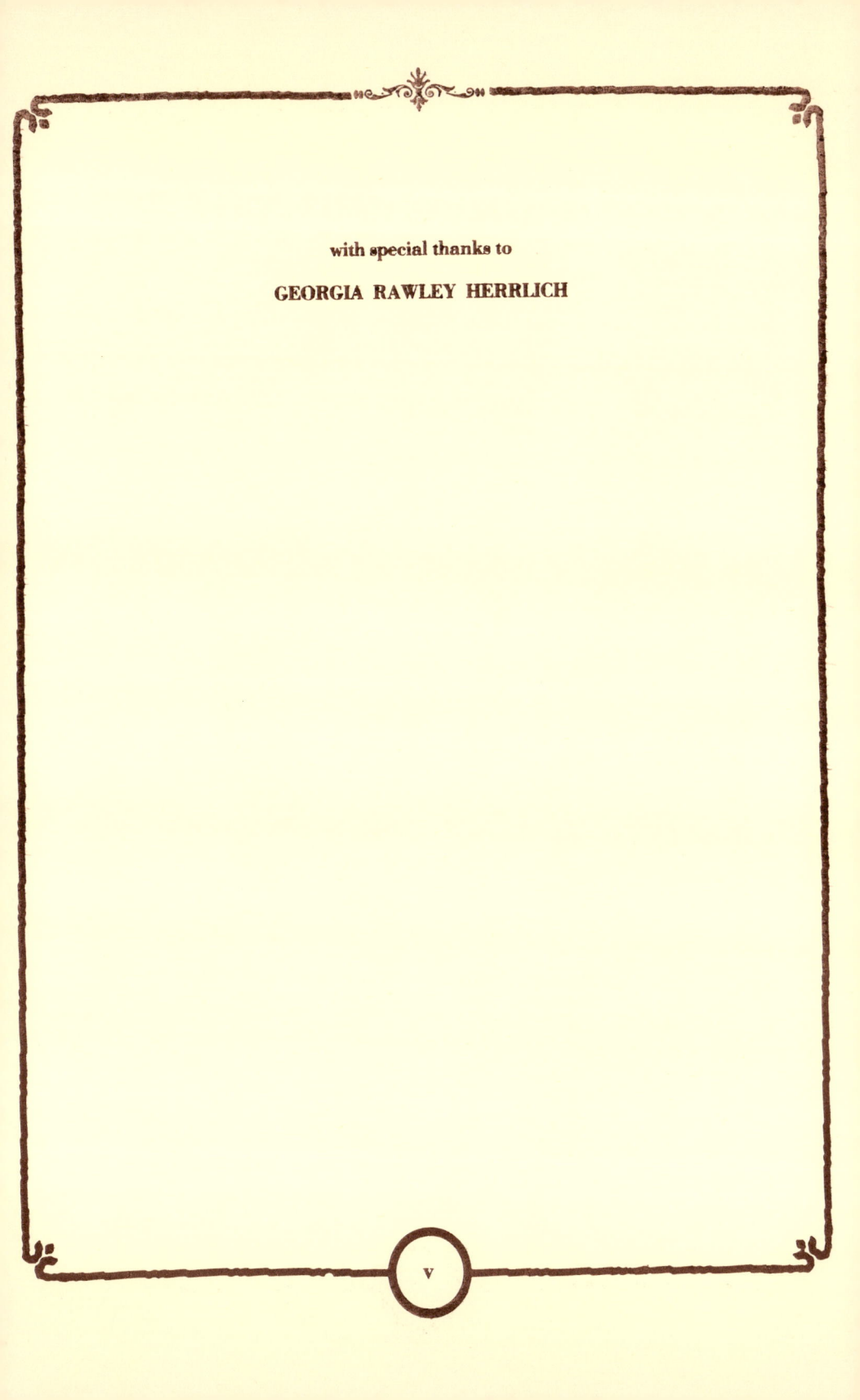

GEORGIA RAWLEY HERRLICH

... having taken
but a whit

from the stacks
of your flax

I've spun and I've weaved
I've weaved and I've spun

a bit

into

this little pile

of um . . .

gold

Rumplestiltskin

* FOREWARD *

Forever
gold
seldom glue

ever Never alas

an
occasional few

barren castels & full moons

- in a word
or

out of it -

typical Utopia

everything pleases

nothing
is

surprising

Smoke

rising from burning
waters

curls in clouds

**Sounds effect
sleeps on breezes**

emptyheads

— jugs of naught —

**writhe in whether
(whether or not)**

**children fly
their**

kites & bombers

lets watch

You and I

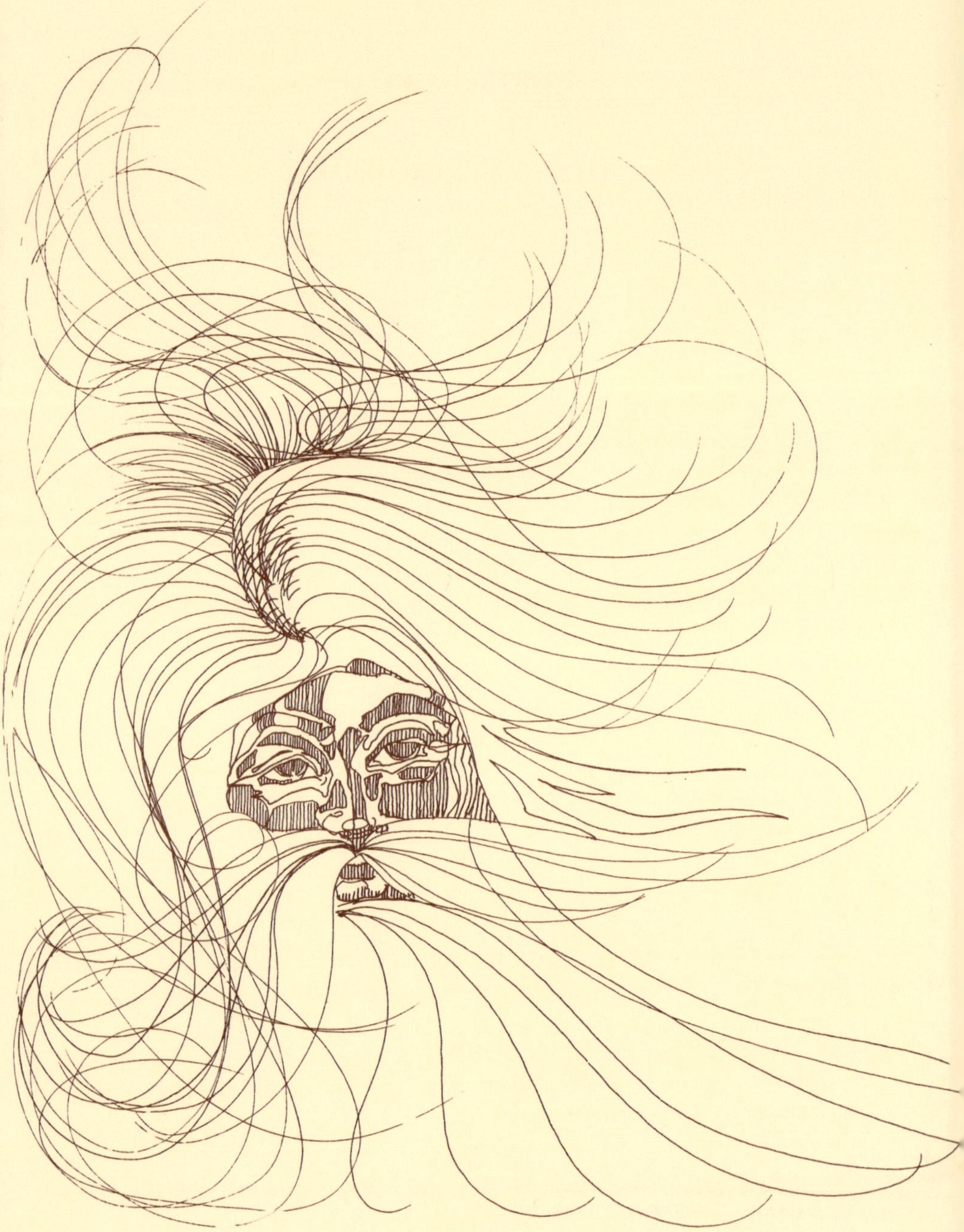

INTRODUCTION

Book

began long before
these
countless chapters
— written at random —

more
will be told

granting
the Time grows
ripe

(and
my mind
thinks less
of
myself & plans
yet to write)

or
ambitions progress
from
my heart to
reach my hands

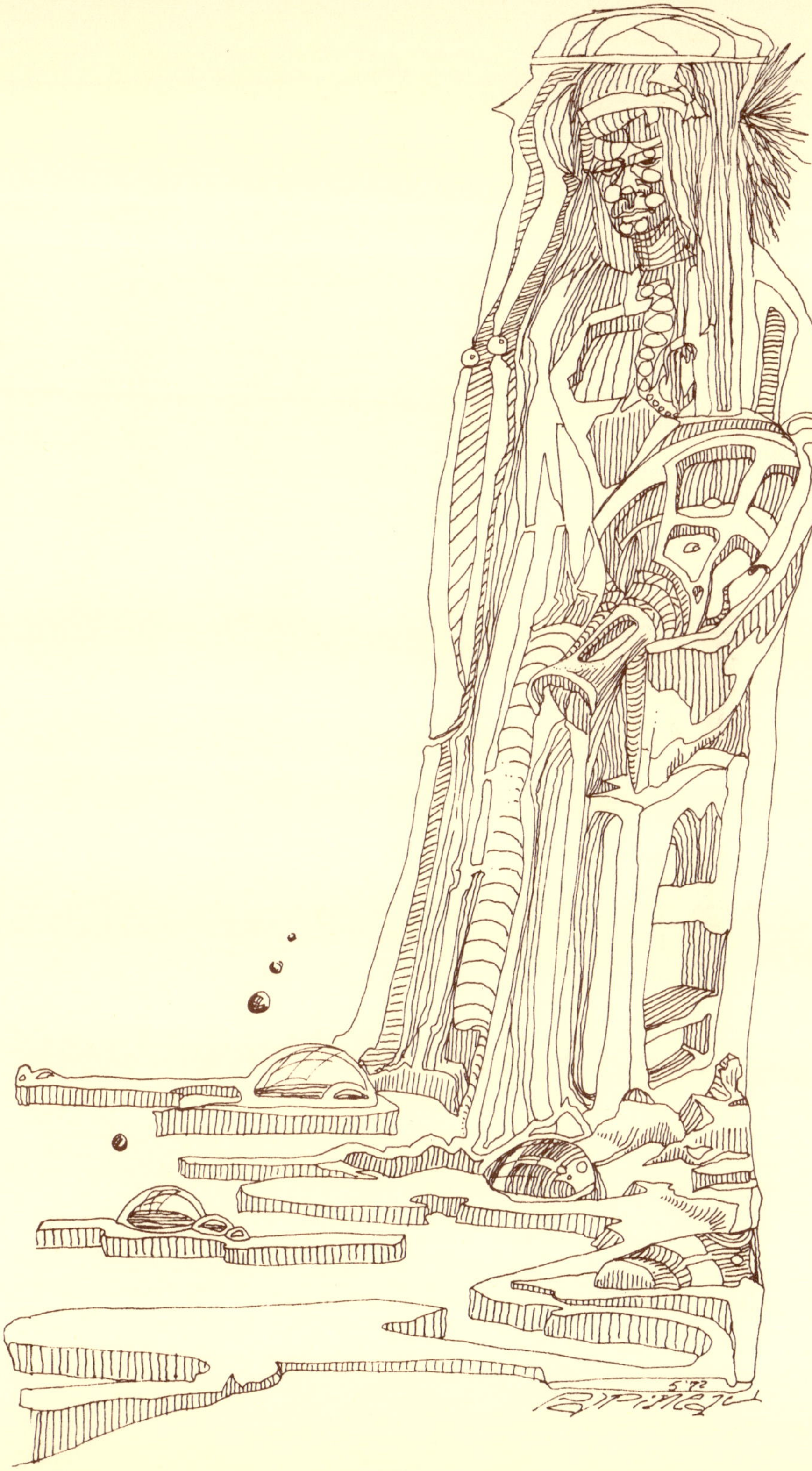

CONTENTS

NOTE FROM A HELPING HAND vii
FOREWARD viii
INTRODUCTION xi
CONTENTS xiv

PREMONITION 1
MODERN CONVENIENCE 2
THE DAY WILL COME 5
A WINDSONG BLEW 11
[THE] HORRIBLE MUSEUM 13
TRANSITION GENERATION 16
THANKS . . . BUT NO THANKS 18
    MYTHING HONOR AMONG THIEVES
FOUND IN A LOG 22
TESTIMONY 26
ALPHABET SOUP 28

THE PREGNANT POMEGRANATE	31
DANCE OF THE DELICATE ELEPHANT	37
LEGEND ?	43

BLISS	48
LATELY	50
NICE WEATHER	53
DIVERSION EXCURSION	57
FROM NOWHERE TO NOWHEN	62

ID SAL ID	69
— OR — A LIST OF WORDS I WANT TO FORGET	
ZiiS	74
ATAVISM	78
REFLECTION	85
MIDNIGHT SONATA	87
JUDGEMENT DAY	91
A CONTINUAL ELSEWHERE FANTASY	94
MIRAGE	97

AFTERWORD	100
EPILOGUE	102

* PREMONITION *

Do
not waver
over
what you may
discover —
What would it be like
if
you already knew...

MODERN CONVENIENCE

A
suicide booth & sterilization
center

left right

on
the street

first here
then

there

A
simple booth
with
an 'OFF' button
easy to find

open to the public
In case of emergency —

break
the
ties that bind

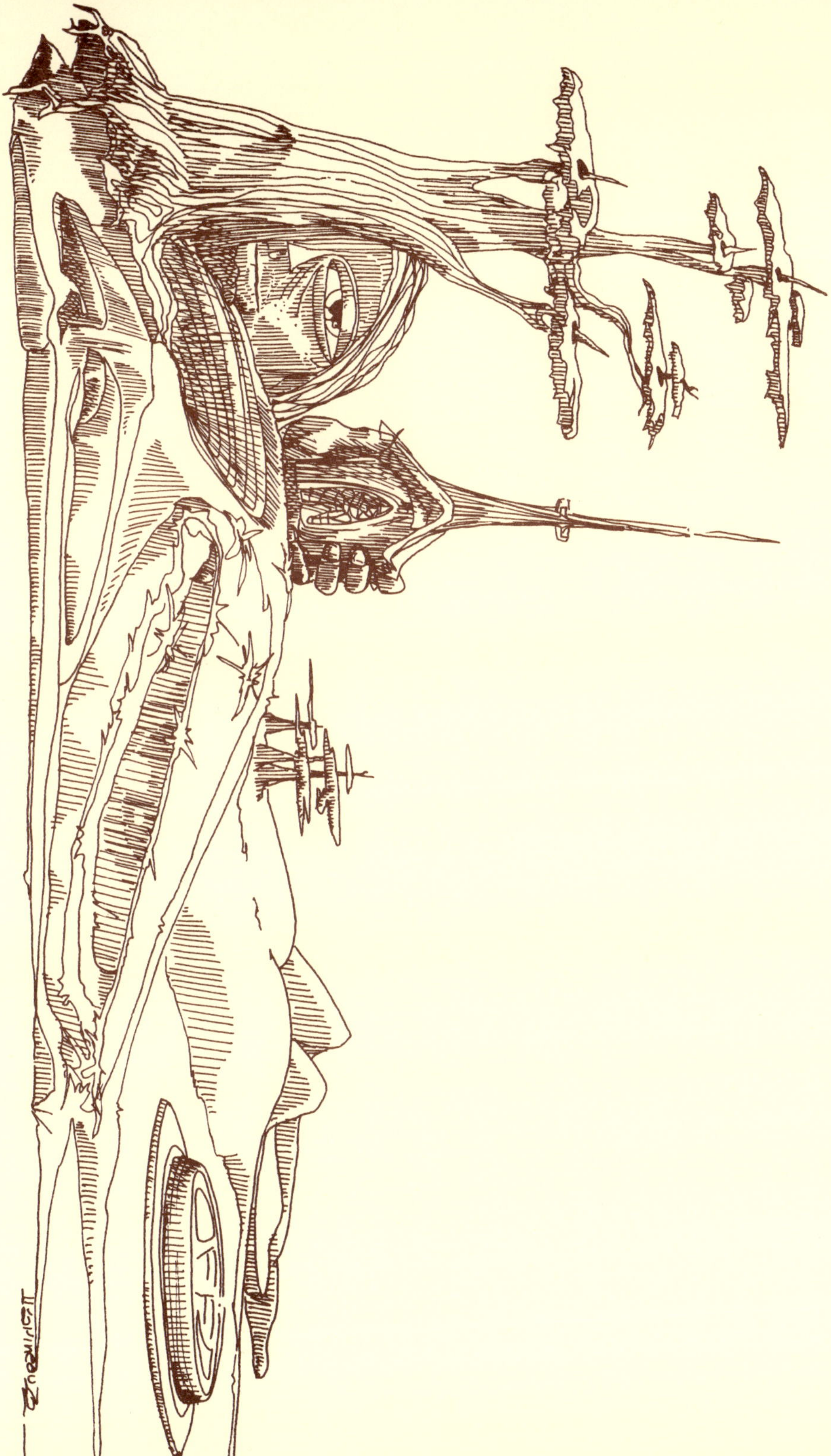

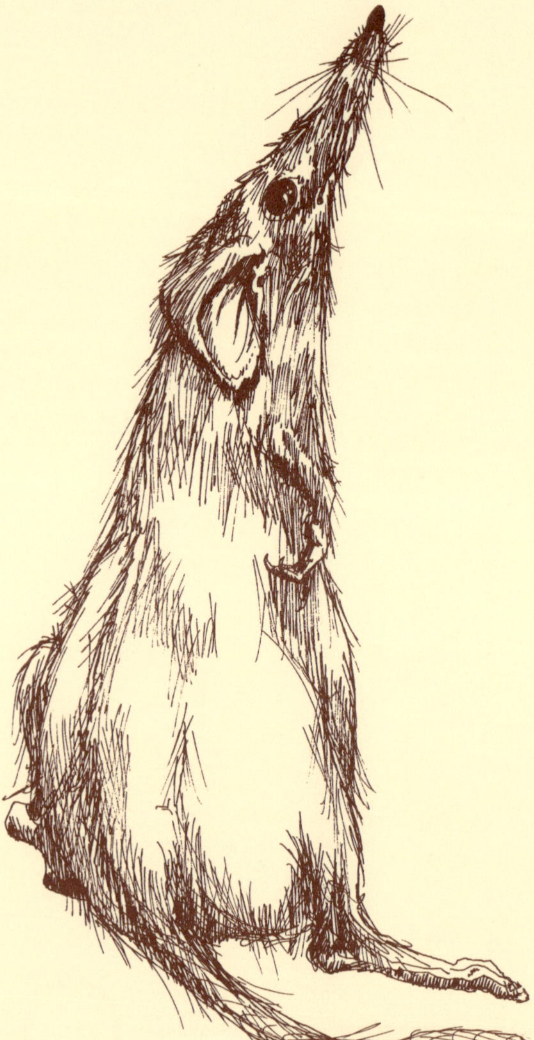

THE DAY WILL COME

when . . .

your Spirit tries
to
rattle itself
free

from your cage

to
contemplate its leavings

— as one would
a
conundrum —

while . . .

Flamingos and Polar Bears
romp
about
the
hazy gray ends

that lie beyond

local horizons

the
Fence
they build

to keep us

out

begins
to keep them

in

Secrets

treasured and guarded

till now —

no longer apply

somehow . . .

the
achievement
of

our Being here

vibrates
in
Space

provided

for the nonce

A
special place —

every
face

everywhere

you should go

the
way
stretching cobwebs

&

vacant moments

can

fill

with

numb

wait

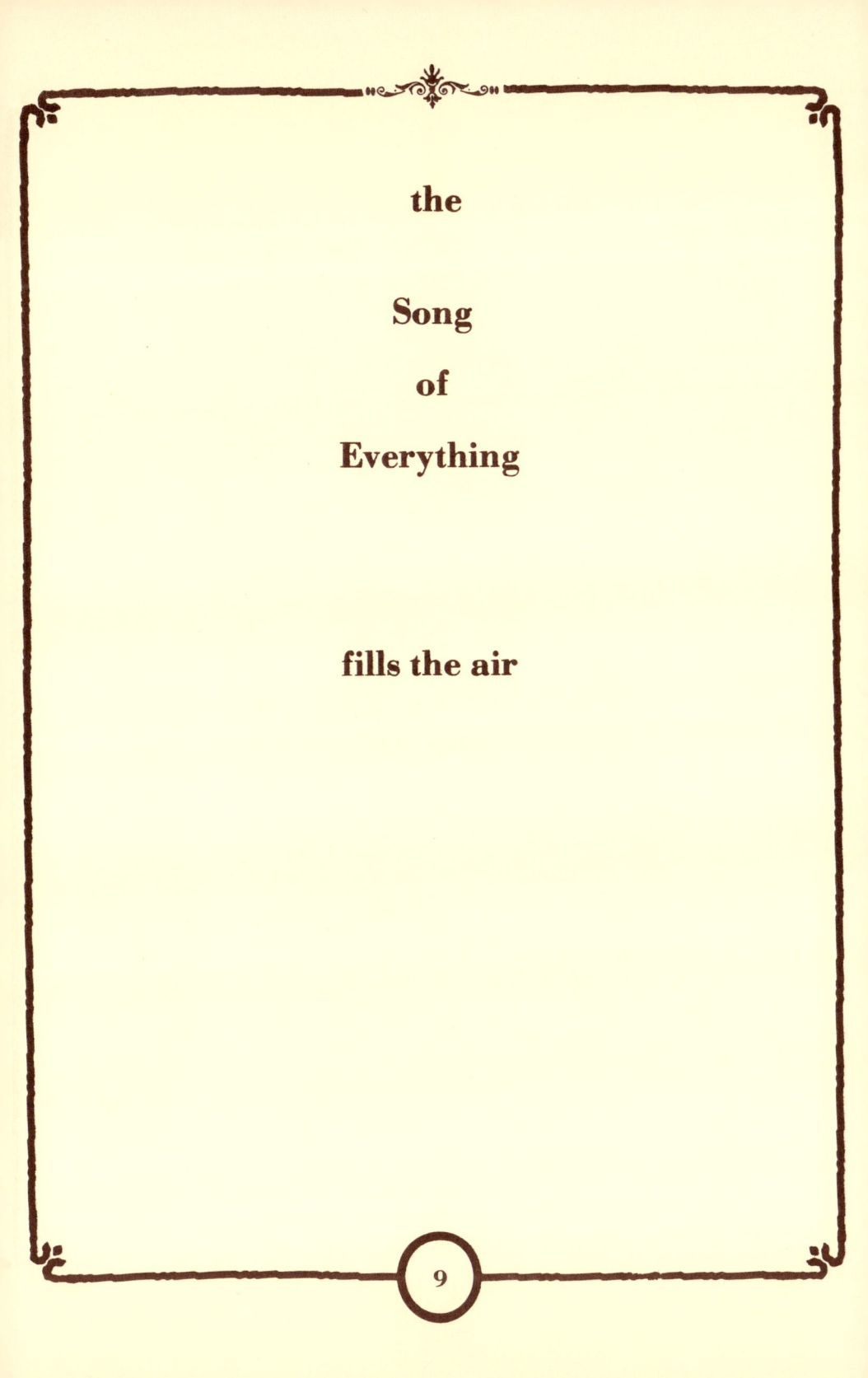

the

Song

of

Everything

fills the air

A WINDSONG BLEW

I
noticed a melody

that
rose from a flower

amber

idyll
lyric
passed my ear

glowing
as a cloud

drifting
across a phase
in the
Moon

Tho'
I've read them
still

all those words
are new

a song of blue

here

**hairy and hairless
hands**

reach across

Time and almost

**touch
each other**

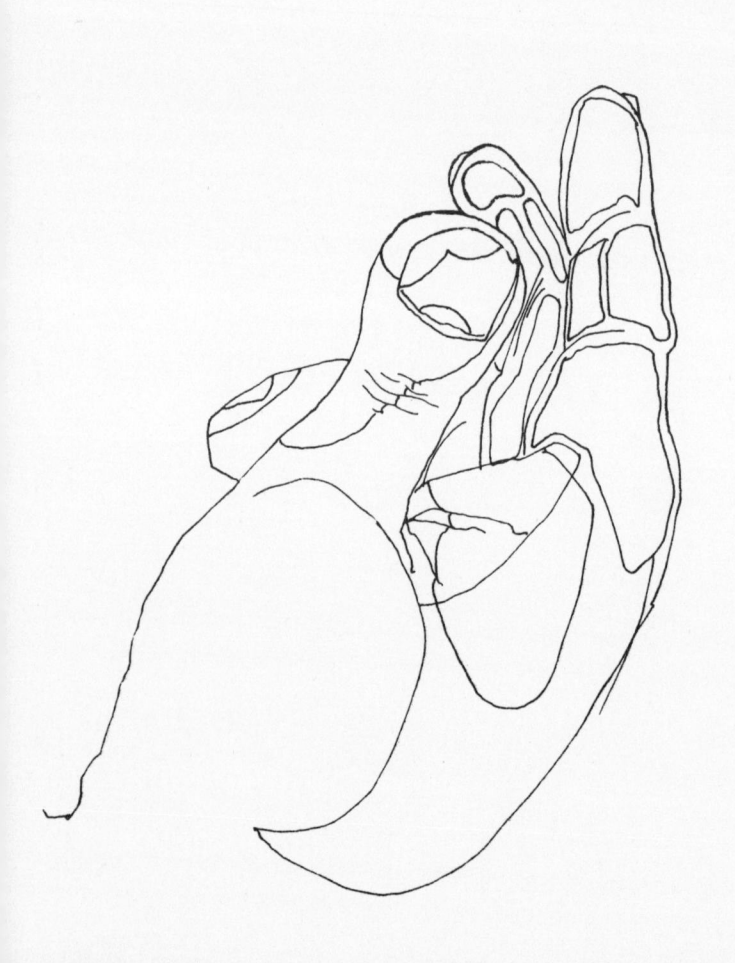

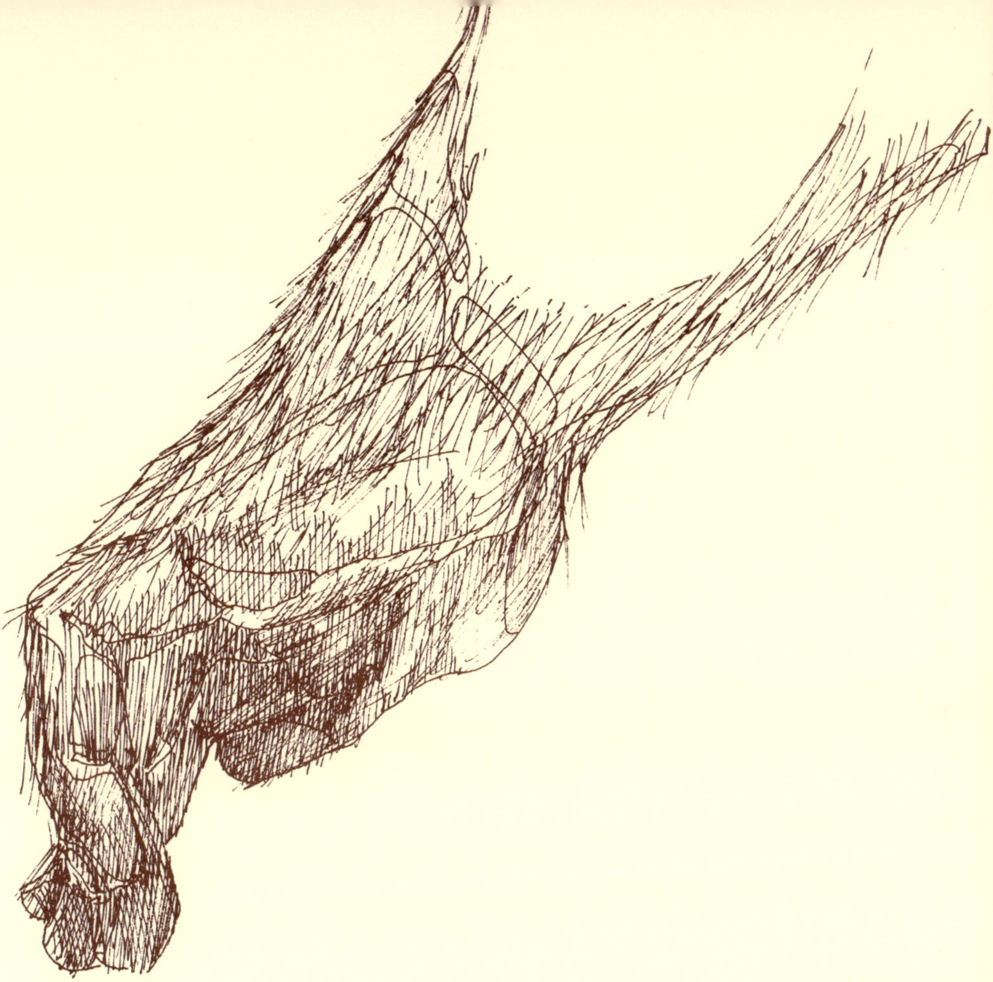

generating

giants

Titans

parents of the gods

before
TV
and

thenceforth

how few

we are

Now

this old

that

knew

THANKS . . . BUT NO THANKS
MYTHING HONOR AMONG THIEVES

fleeing
Sherwood Forest

a barefoot pair
with
flapping capes

singing epithets
to
Robin Hood
in

two-part harmony

. . . he's a scoundrel
he's a rascal
he's a robber
he's a freak . . .

arrive at a conclusion

— there's no place
like home —

saith
the Count

(of Monte Cristo)

to
the Scarlet Pimpernel

I heard
my castle

calling

a hearth
awaits
with open fire

patient porridge
in the
pantry

keeps faith

with
appetite's desire

Would you care
to hang

your hat there
sire?

Count M.C. —
(replies the 'Scar')

coral grows

not

on the tide
nor

on the shore

But

fills the gap

'tween

ocean wave and ocean floor

with

reefs

&

hulls of sunken ship

and

keyholes
without doors

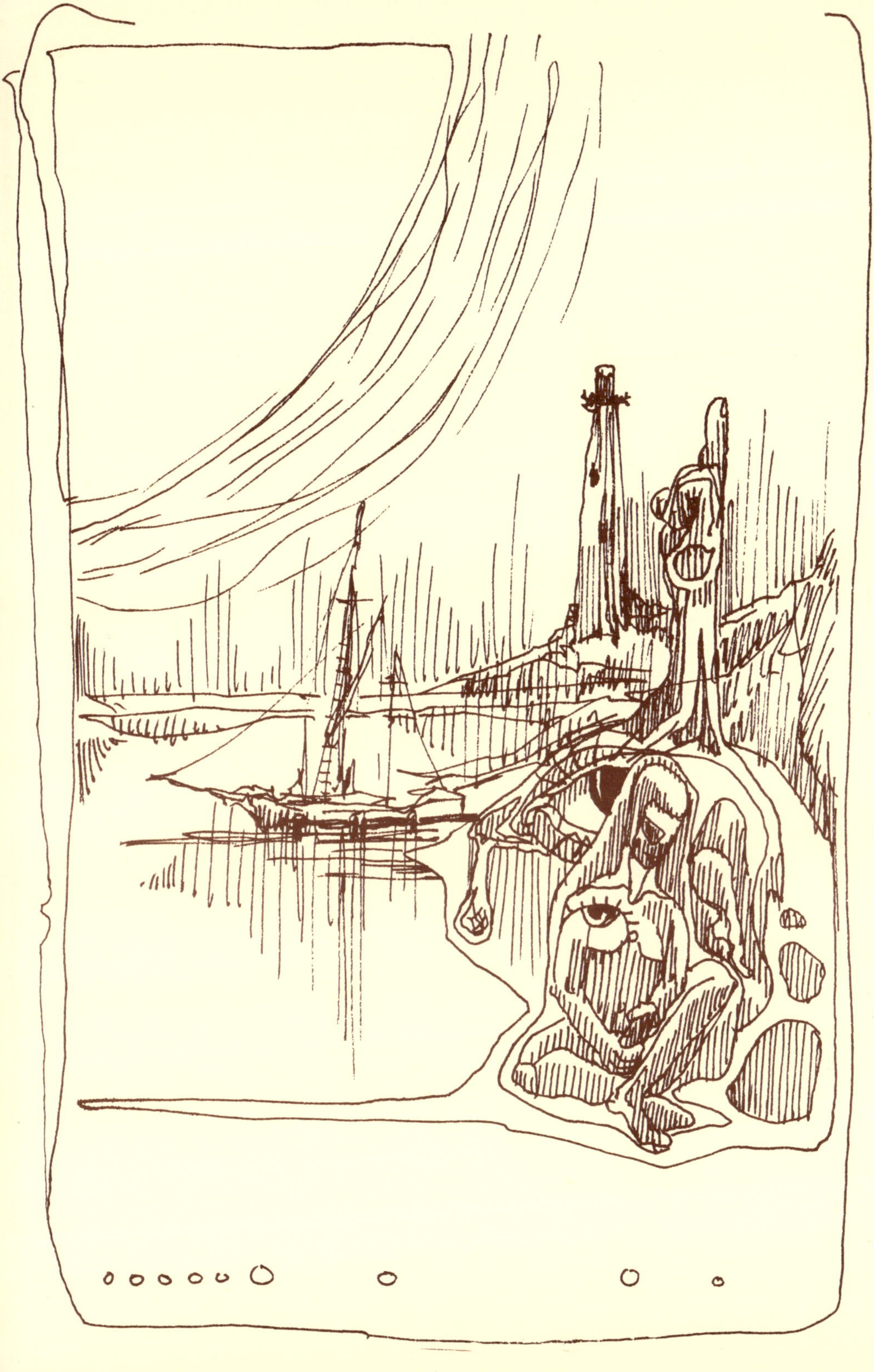

FOUND IN A LOG

Like
a stranger
drifting with the current

I drew nigh
the
face
of an
enchanted
swamp
by
eventide

Silhouettes and Birdcalls
midst
the tender haze
of
timeless mists

grown
from the bog
on the horizon
with
the distance melting
away

I did hear

Where
finely
Jeweled dew

clinging and dripping

on the
Whole

scents the atmosphere
with
pleasant perfume

I
smile at my
compass
and
fill in my map

with a song

carefully
marking
the

aria

when I buried

memorabilia

among the roots
of a

gnarled
mind

and

laughed in colors

no one
would ever guess

exist

I
wouldn't
change
the
way
I've
lived

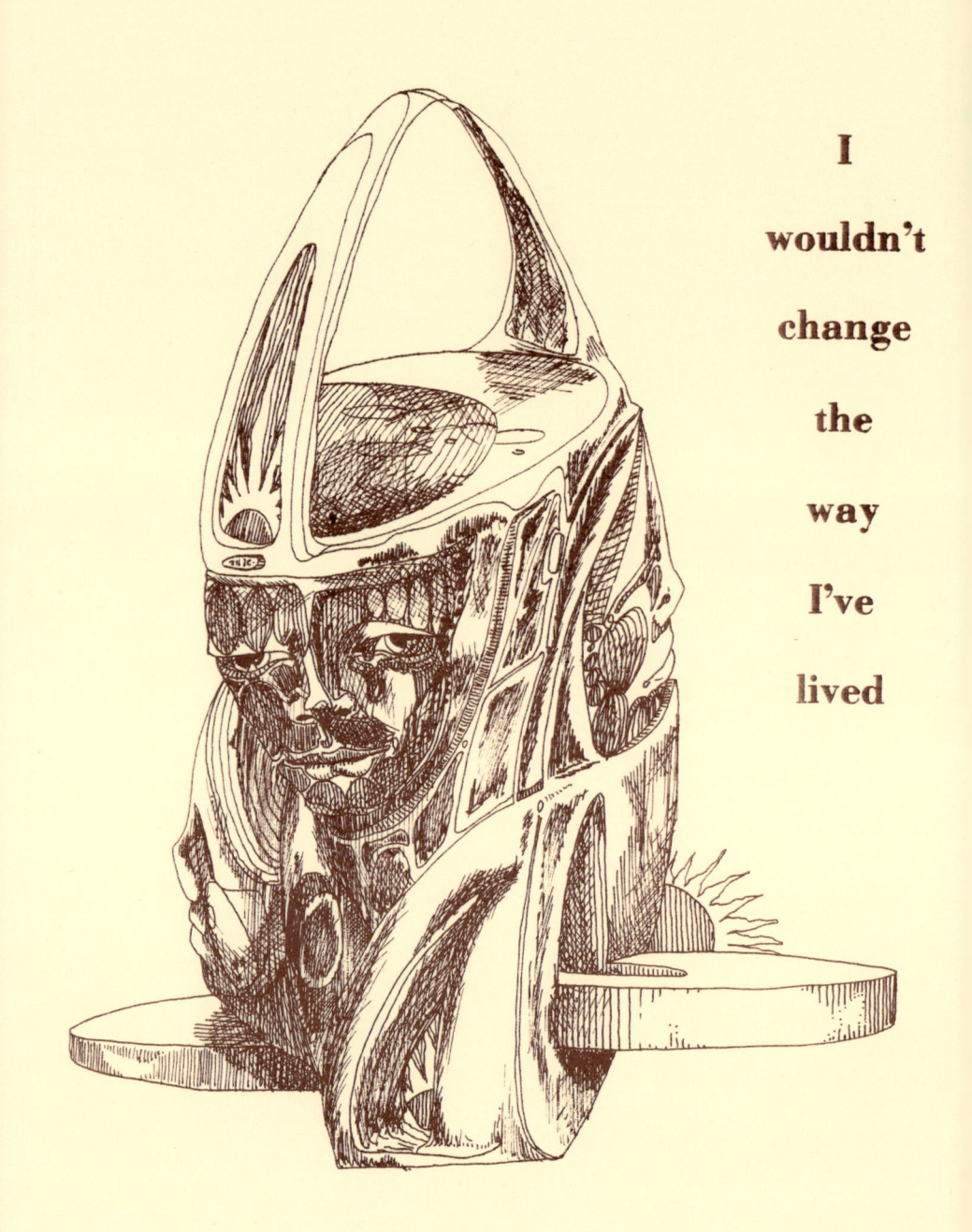

I
AM

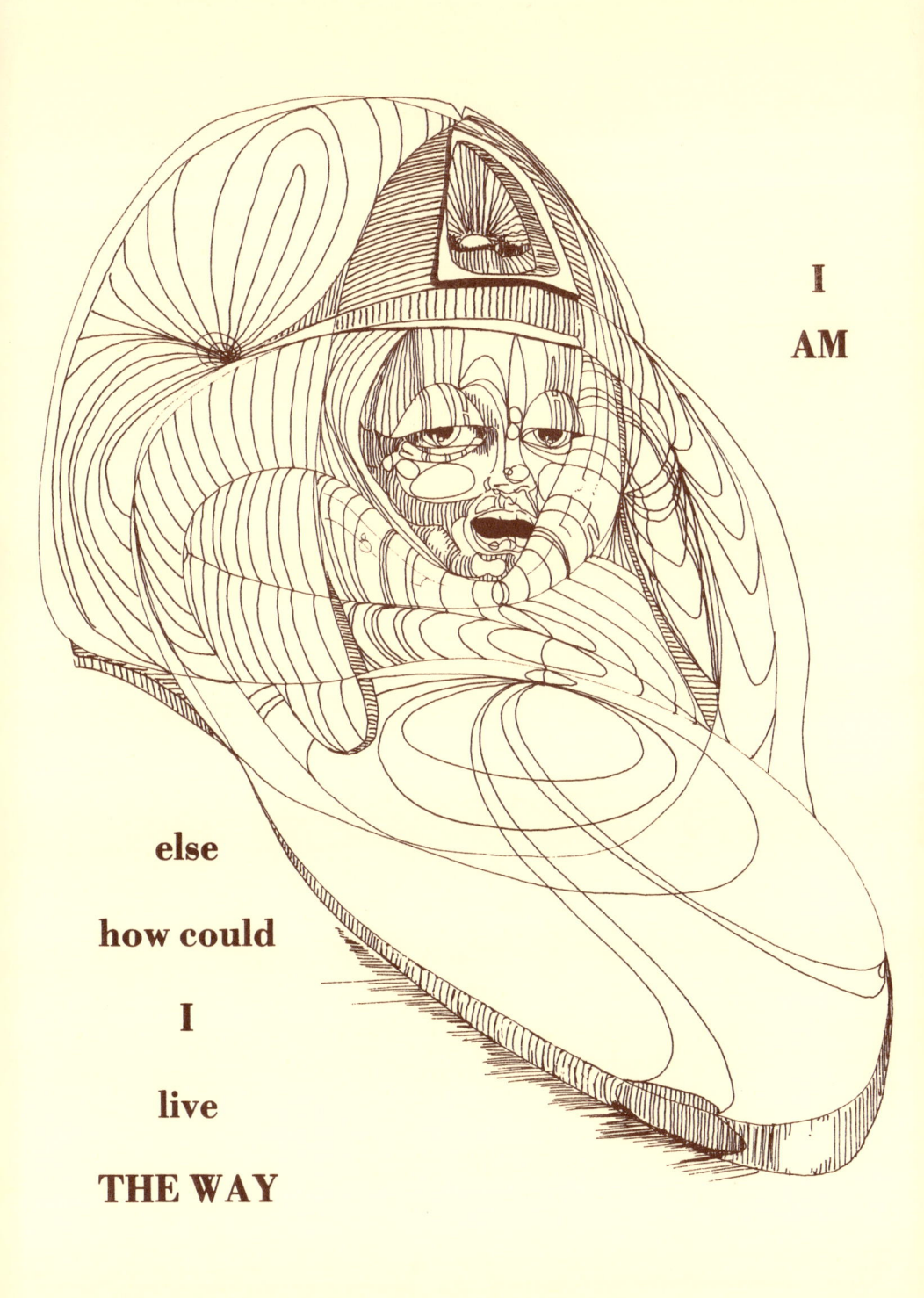

else

how could

I

live

THE WAY

ALPHABET
ALPHABET
ALPHABET

Soup

what

funny

Languages

to eat

to eat

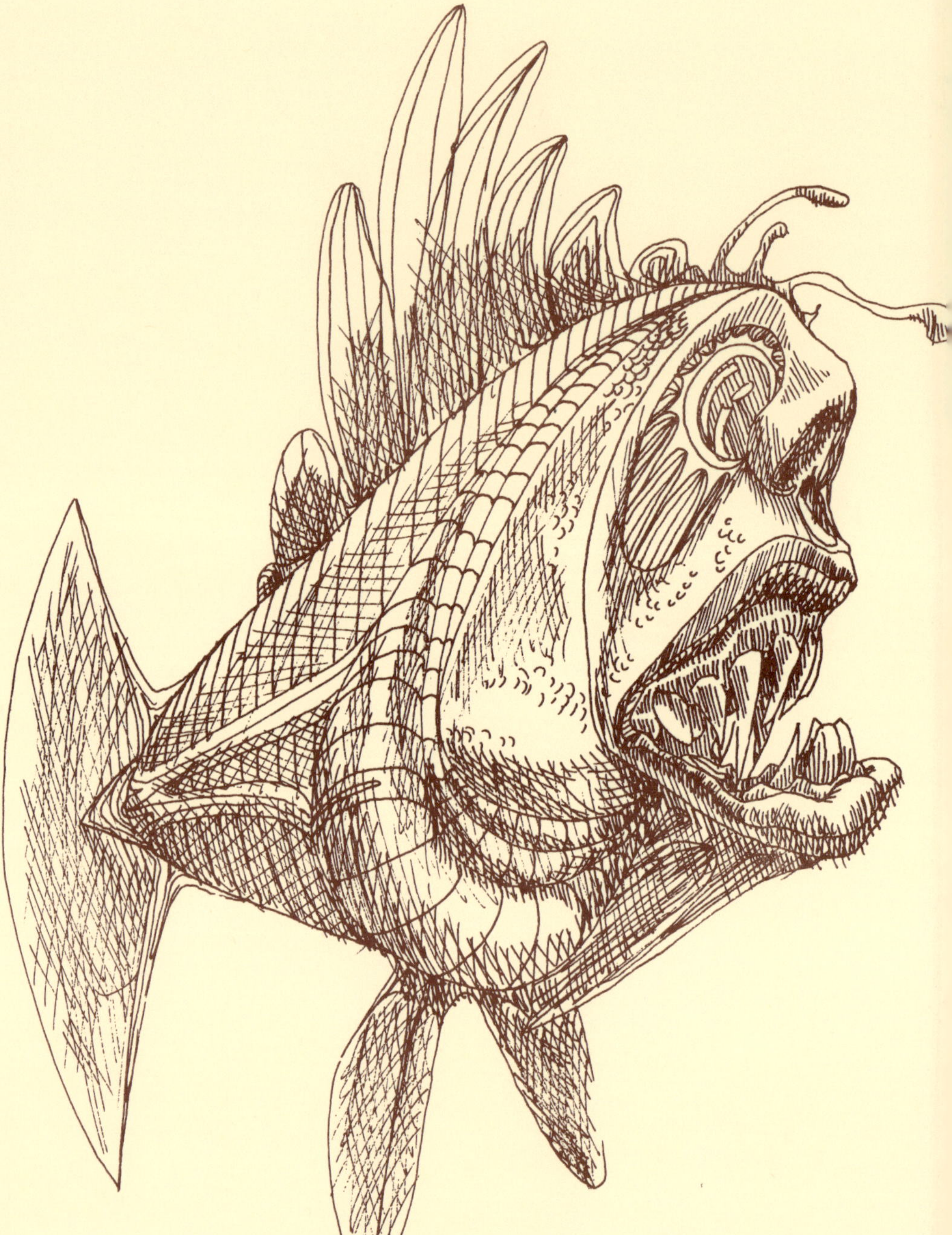

✴ THE PREGNANT POMEGRANATE ✴

A
pomegranate

bursting

its
succulent seeds'
trajectories

set

a
Sun
giving birth:

to

planets & debris*

*Space
isn't space
unless
its empty

is it?

an
Eye
fogged by grit
like prejudice

distorts reality

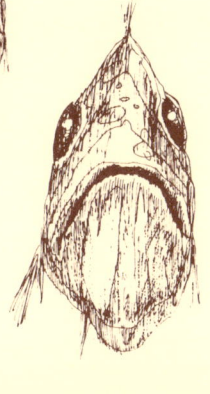

(let not
the limits of
awareness
deny
existence)

for instance...

A
boxful of night

—— captured ——

to be
viewed & studied
at

noon

Excitement
over

—— successfully ——

removing his head
and
laying the innards
out

soon

makes that

otherwise
non-descript neo-emperic

cross his eyes

when
he
gets himself
together

he'll realize he's

left-handed

A
fish
refuses

to
bathe and gets
put down by
its school

far down

as one can
fathom

**Bare
is a
Tree**
coated

now & then

with
sunshine or snow

this tree

you see
won't leave

you see
his tree

died

Stairs
&
echoes

stars & bloodlines

and
crystal so clear

you can tell

there's

Nothing

on the otherside
nothing

on the otherside

till

Nature

giving up prestige
to
Providence

gives birth
to

a pregnant pomeggranate

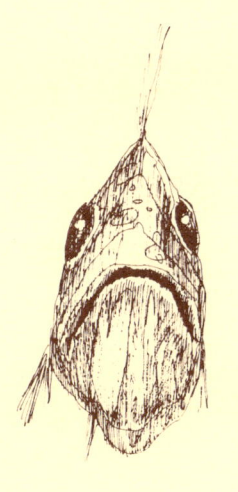

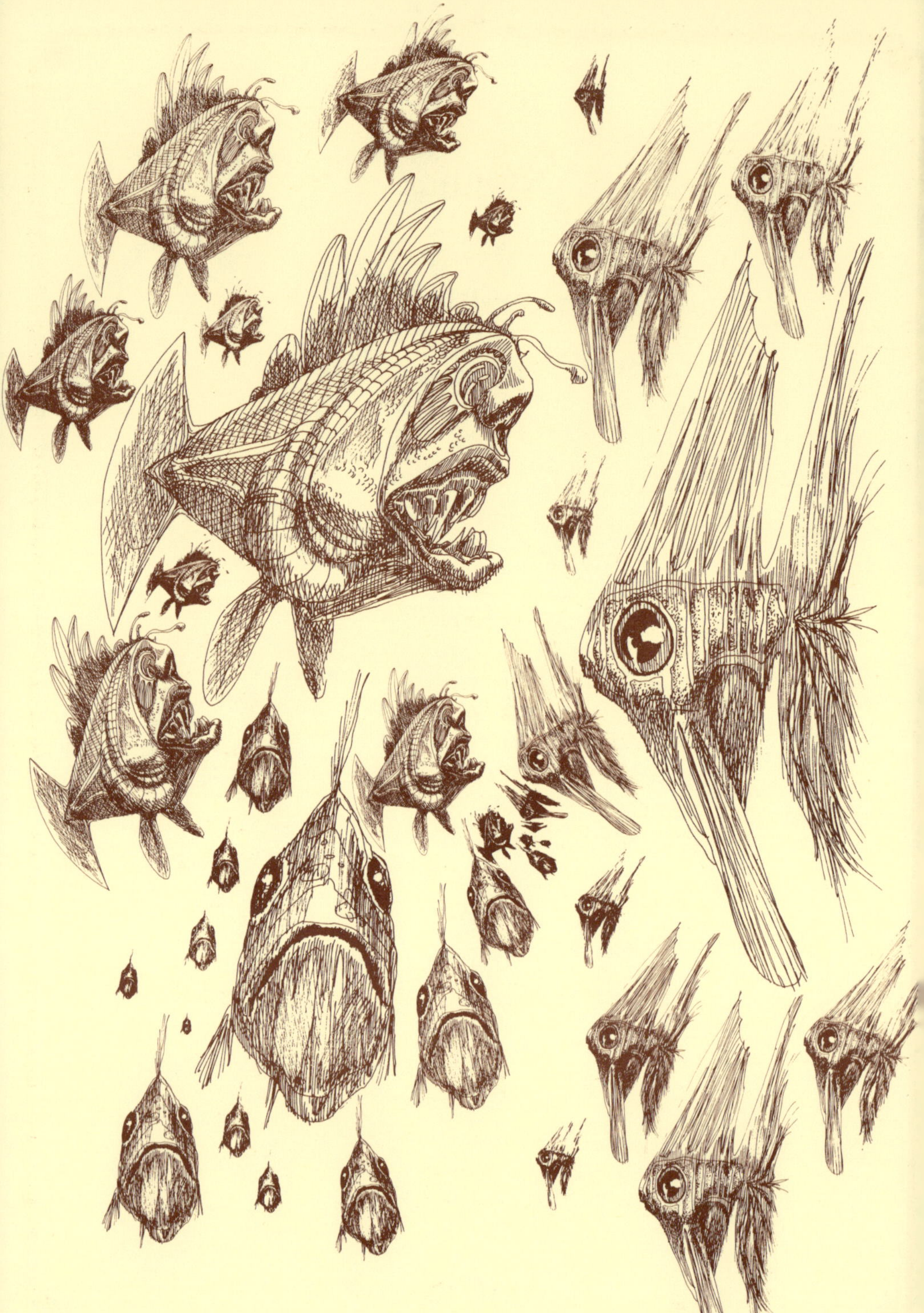

as

Our Sun

beats

down

and

Cores of Snow

melt

in

tune

Cool

attitudes

pass

thru

Fire Archways

none turn back

The
ideal image
of the
flower

is
flung before us
like
steppingstones

of
Time

[while]

Large
tick tocks
of
watch clocking

march along
the
tempo

Rock
abounds
'round

Lillies
of the
Valley

A
canyon
joins a bluff
rising
in
perfect unison
to the
falls
of a
stream

then:

Gulches
filled with glaciers
and
Mountains
gorged themselves
with
earthquakes

[and]

Overlooking a basin

upon a plateau

dances

a

delicate

Elephant

in the

Afterglow

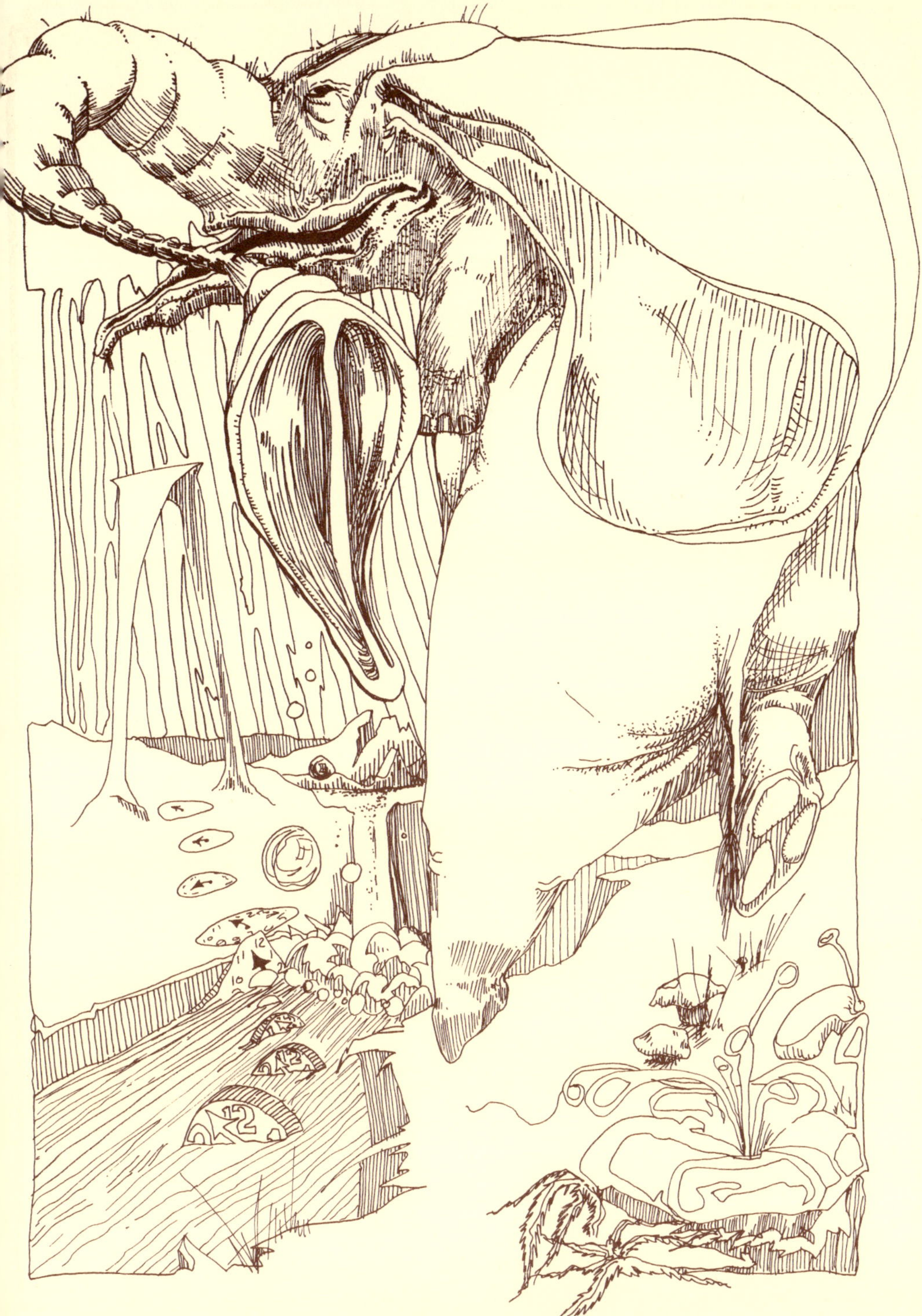

✽ LEGEND ? ✽

Onyx Tarantulas
dressed in braided silver
step
nimbly over lodestone

in a
lost mine
somewhere
not far from
here

The natives tell

— reluctantly —

of a
treasure find

Strange & Rare

in a
lost mine
somewhere
not far from

here

a
Gem

radiating light

glows over bones
of the
fortunate few

who
got Rich quick

in a
lost mine

somewhere

not far from

here

Yonder
'mongst dancing
Joshua and Superstition

whilst a smile
of
Moon
swings

— like a pendulum —

from a star

look

to the

coyote

who cries
of the

Prize

that
lingers & dwindles

in a
lost mine
somewhere

not far from

here

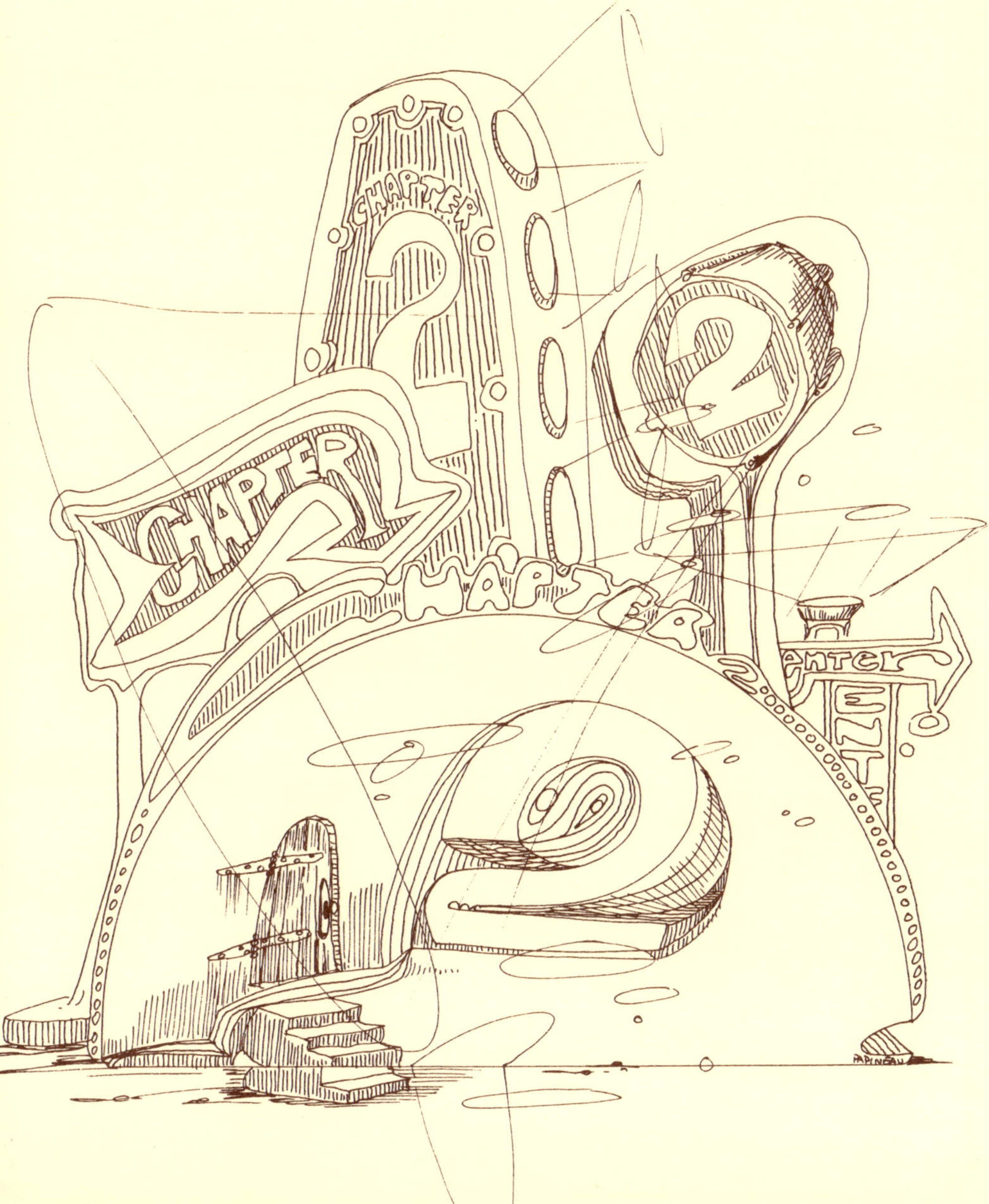
CHAPTER
2
CHAPTER
CHAPTER
2
enter
PAPINEAU

* BLISS *

thy
Sword
&
rebellion

hath
felled the tree
of thy

Hope

and

on
the bed
of
ease

thou layest

in
style

* a fitting fête *

meanwhile

chilled
fire wine

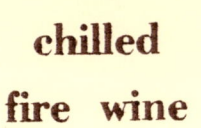

and

eternal fruit

in

Placeless Paradise

await

* LATELY *

Strange days
come to stay
awhile

eating
all the
Time

keeping us busy
waiting on them
to pass

Look ahead

when
all this
will be

a

Memoir

of
nothing to remember
except

mystery & puzzlement

and that
we were

there

together

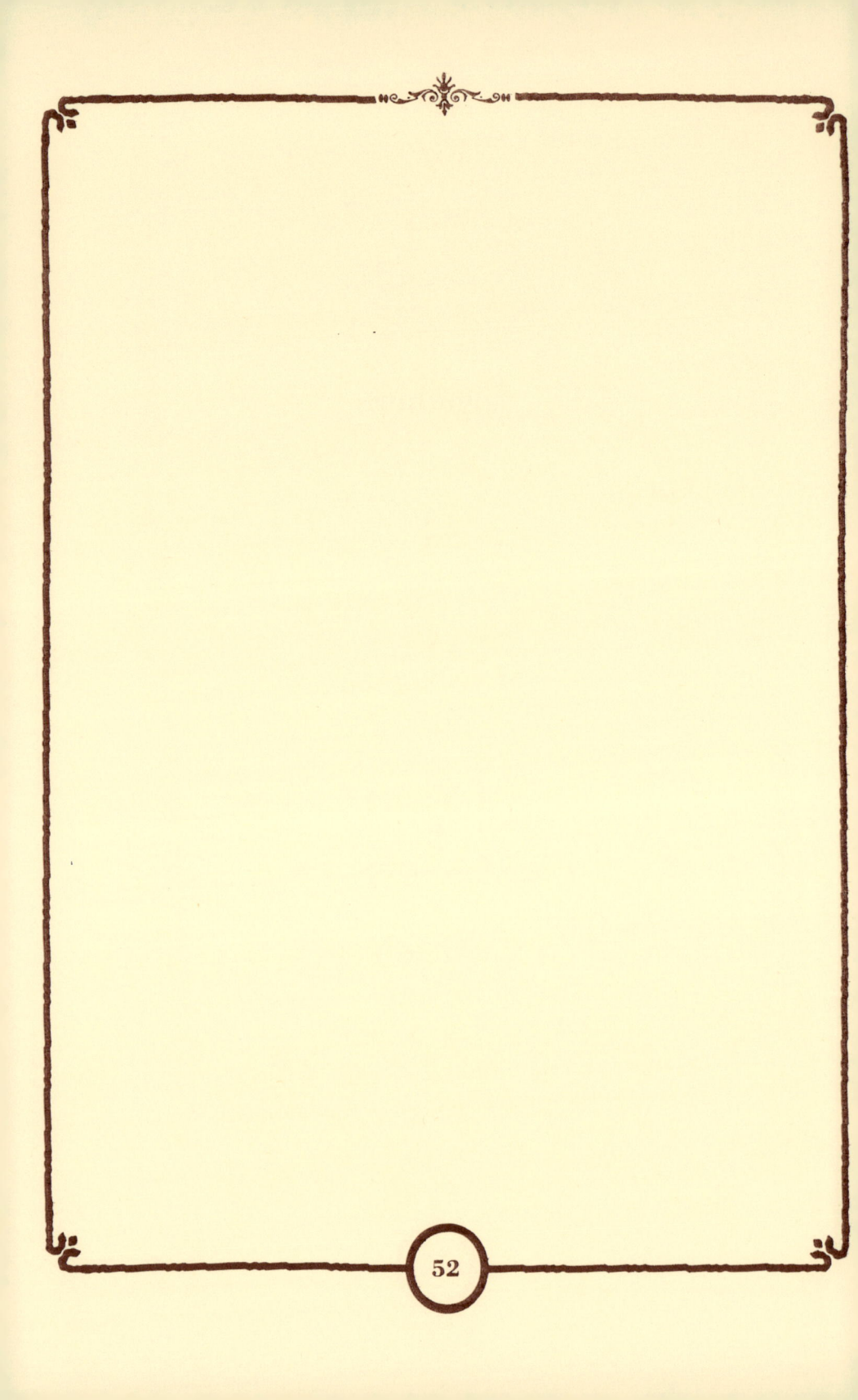

NICE WEATHER

Eve

everybody waits

gray infinity
gives way
to
dark blue

Night

everybody sleeps

unpredictable dreams
end
as expected
in

Morning

everybody begins

the Sun has
its day
then

rests
in the
West

come

Eve

everybody waits

✱ DIVERSION EXCURSION ✱

Strolling
about a Zoo
one day

I
stopped
this moment

near some shade

watching
a
pit of fears

[After]

thoughtlessly feeding
the
lemurs

bears & things

I

saw

a couple
eagles:

Bald

In glass
enclosures
several sicknesses
lay

I didn't stay

Just outside
a
new exhibit
gathered quite a crowd

An inscription
over a bar
announced the feature:

W̶ORLD'S ONLY

KNOWN

CAPTIVE

Invisible Creature

what a truly

indelible

Sound

✱ FROM NOWHERE TO NOWHEN ✱

gaunt

Griffin
guardians

of
sources for treasures

meander thru catacombs

dragging
heavy dreambags

calling
'New Pleasures'

— undiluted madness

reflected

by

unabashed mirrors —

Fabulous Monster
with

blood of luminous hue

may be seen
where
it is
not

resting
on a nest
of
great stones

Yestereve Dancer
arrived
with the fog

departed
as the storm
broke

wearing only

a
see-thru cloak

**Child
of the
Earth**

creates & dissolves

**the
unchangeable**

Dragon of Rebirth

**divides
the
continuous**

into

cycles & seasons . . .

I

the ruler of
the
Kingdom

of
myself

for
better or worse

— wandering
thru a forest
of
illusion —

be

nourished

by

the central fire

of

Universe

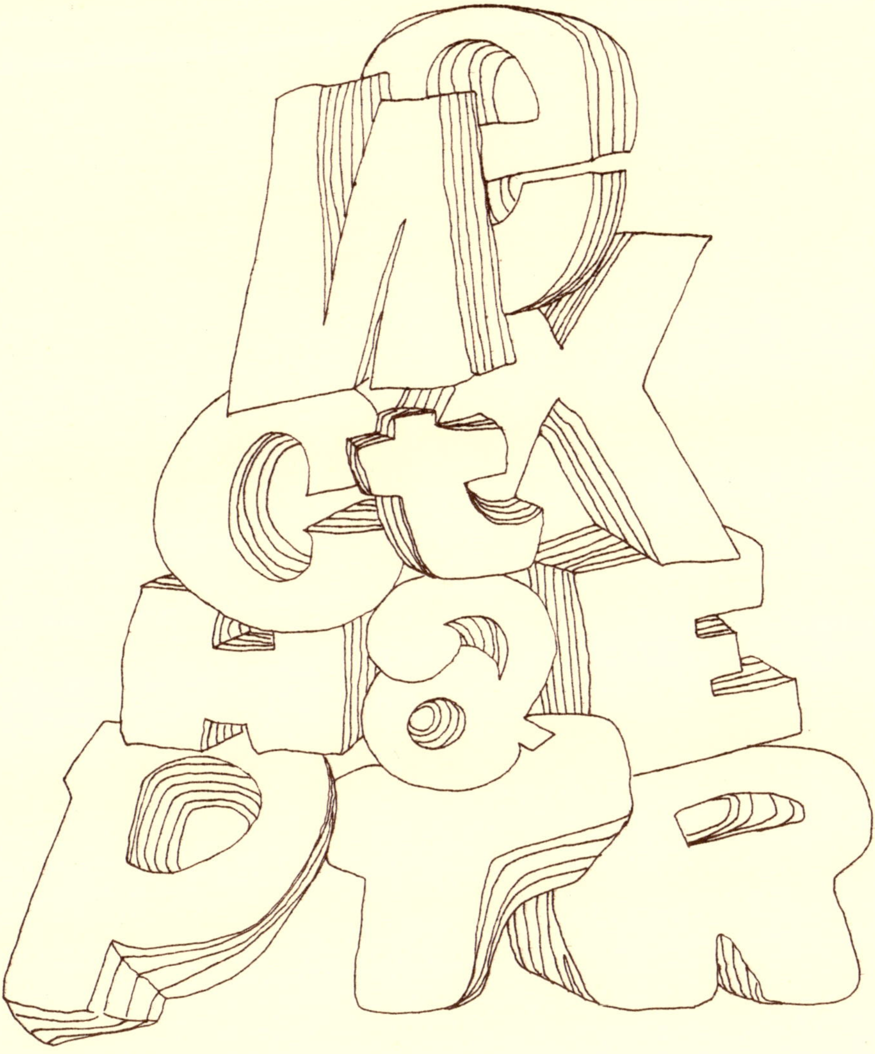

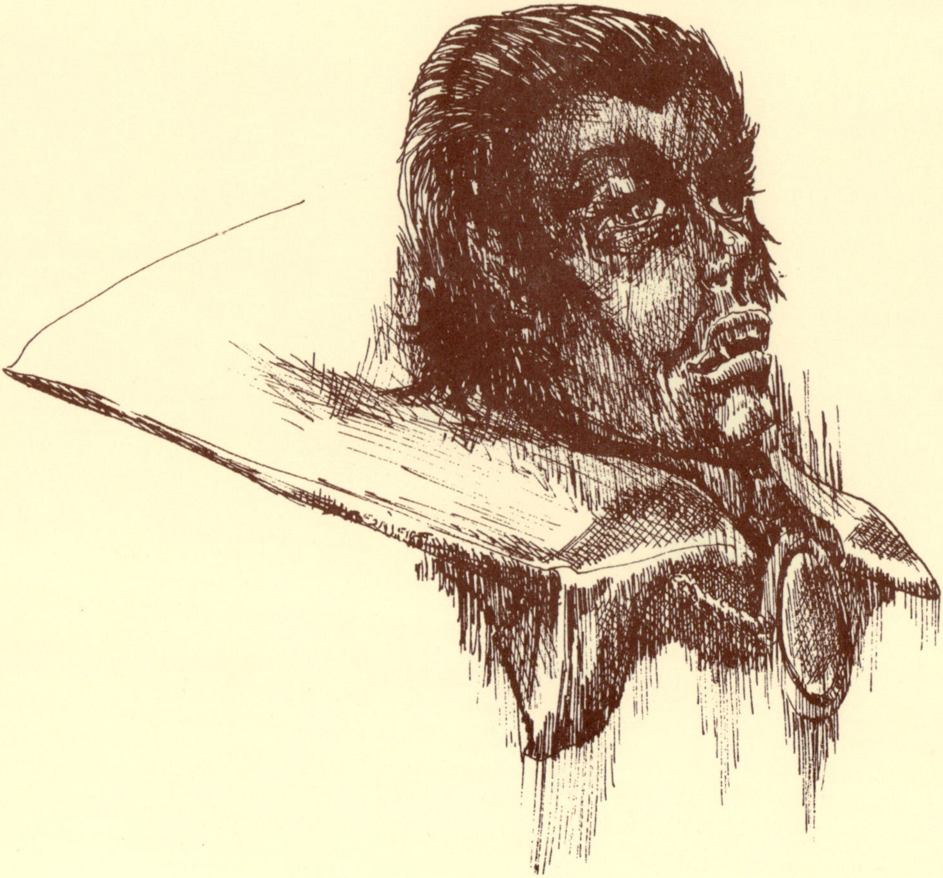

ID SAL ID
— OR —
A LIST OF WORDS I WANT TO FORGET

Soft tambourines

twinkle 'gainst

the

light

nonchalant noise

in a

haphazard

quiet

Highways

wending among signs

and

omens

wrap about us

the ribbon of

our

Deeds

— skeleton
of
our intentions

ghosts
of
our promise —

Important trivia . . .

definitions
from

the Meaningless Dictionary

a collection of
words

meant for

oblivion:

**laughter
from the unamused**

**feasts
before the fasting**

**votes
by absentees**

**Essentials
of the
unnecessary —**

misapplied presumption

**vague fantasies
subtle chaos**

vanishing cream

**— neglected oceans
getting dusty —**

[see note]

[note]

words
are mispelled

except

those
I make up

ZiiS

Here

— tho'
hardly —

this
intensly transparent
next to the last

Where

of
little
&
revolving

Systems

hiding

within the halo
glow

they've cast

Each

of a

name

unpronounceable

to the

Others —

surround & circle

particles

less than atoms

— seeds of Life

cosmic eggs —

particles

less than atoms

— seeds of Life

cosmic eggs —

Primitive Spacecraft

its

true blooded

&

erudite

pilot

a

doomed

yet

stalwart

heart

drifts

toward lunacy

'Beware
the
Science of Fire'

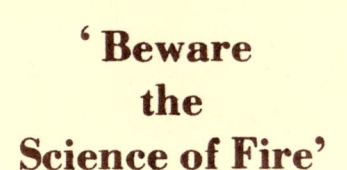

he has
graven
upon
a

key

to

forbidden sanctuaries

— harbors of secrets
for the
reinvention
of

shadows and supremacy —

Ancient Travelier
— bold and curious —

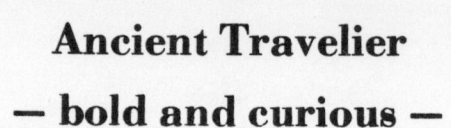

a
minor example
of
extraordinificence

tell
of
superior ancestors

(who knew their origin)

building
shelters & caves
for

outcasts

conventional assumptions

and
backward segments

**Temporal
certainties
of**

universal dread

regard
the
vile & pernicious
wasteland

inhabited with its secret —

[beyond
the Gate of the Sun
between
the Remote and the Elite]

as

an affliction

looked upon
with
favor

the

disintegration

of

Antimatter

that

blows your body

away

leaving

your

Spirit

naked

✱ REFLECTION ✱

You

smoke your way

'long

the narrow street

thru

a tunnel of shadows

pass your feet

there's more to be had

than can be bought

like a Spaceman

in a junkyard

'tis darker

than you

thought

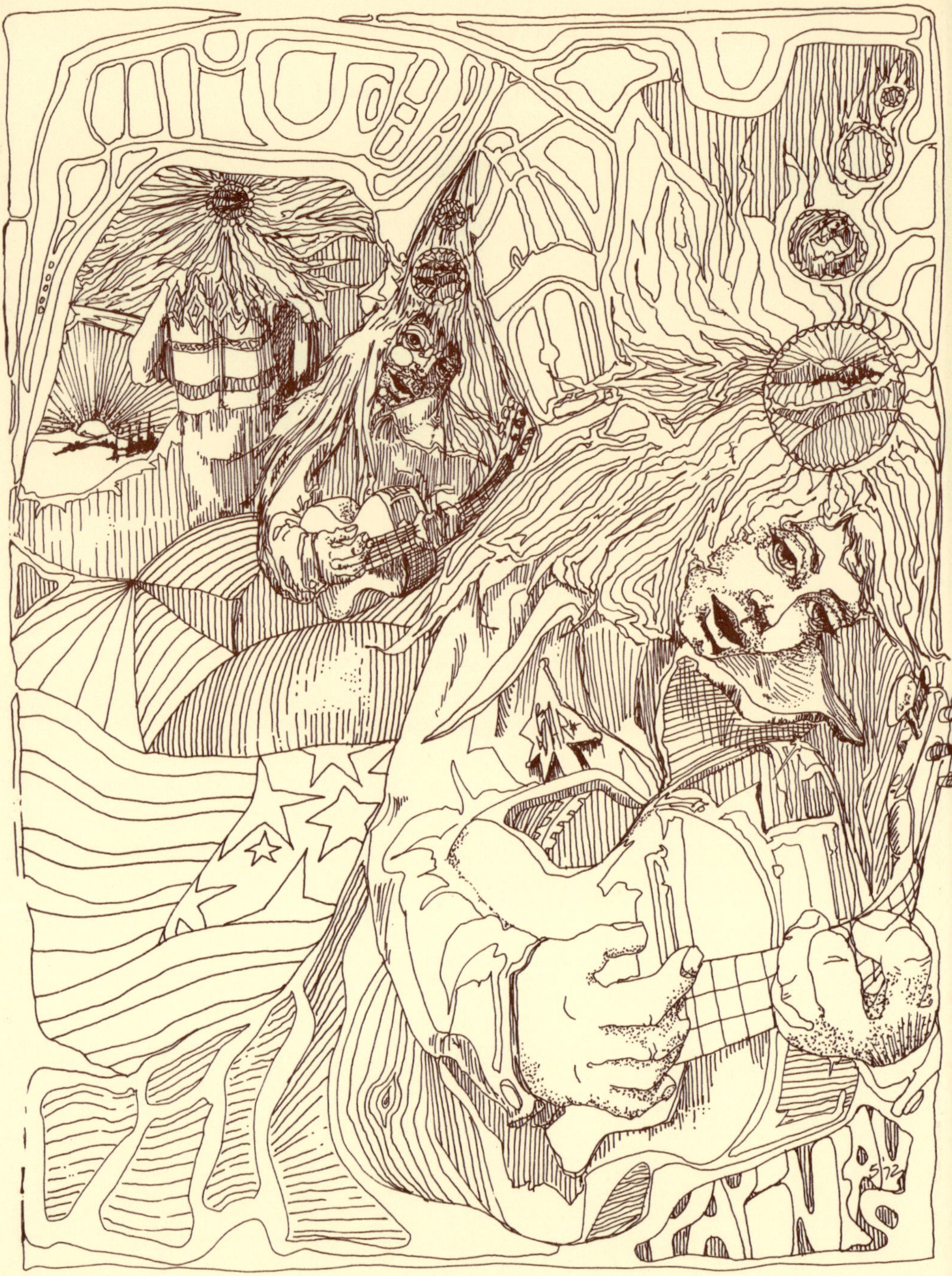

MIDNIGHT SONATA

This
fine empty
suitcase

once full

of
Time and memories

lies
forgotten

with

broken lock and
torn travel tag

names

that fade

like

the twelfth strike

of

Midnight

this
Graveyard
waiting
to swallow us

merely smiles
with
flowered cheek

a
Garden

soon to fade
from sight
and

me & thee

and

the twelfth strike
of
Midnight

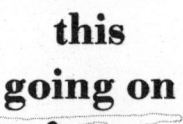

this
going on
from
day to day

our

Endless Journey

will not
stop

Mountains

in the way
will fade

like

daylight

before

the twelfth strike

of

Midnight

✻ **JUDGEMENT DAY** ✻

Fabulous Towers
leaning and bent
with

Jewels

dripping from open
portals

— like blood —

gathering in pools
at
Natural Pearl Foundations

— know what I mean? —

and then . . .

emerges

the
Sun

from

its
eclipse

— an eye
that winked —

its
Light

naively illuminating

the
different

World

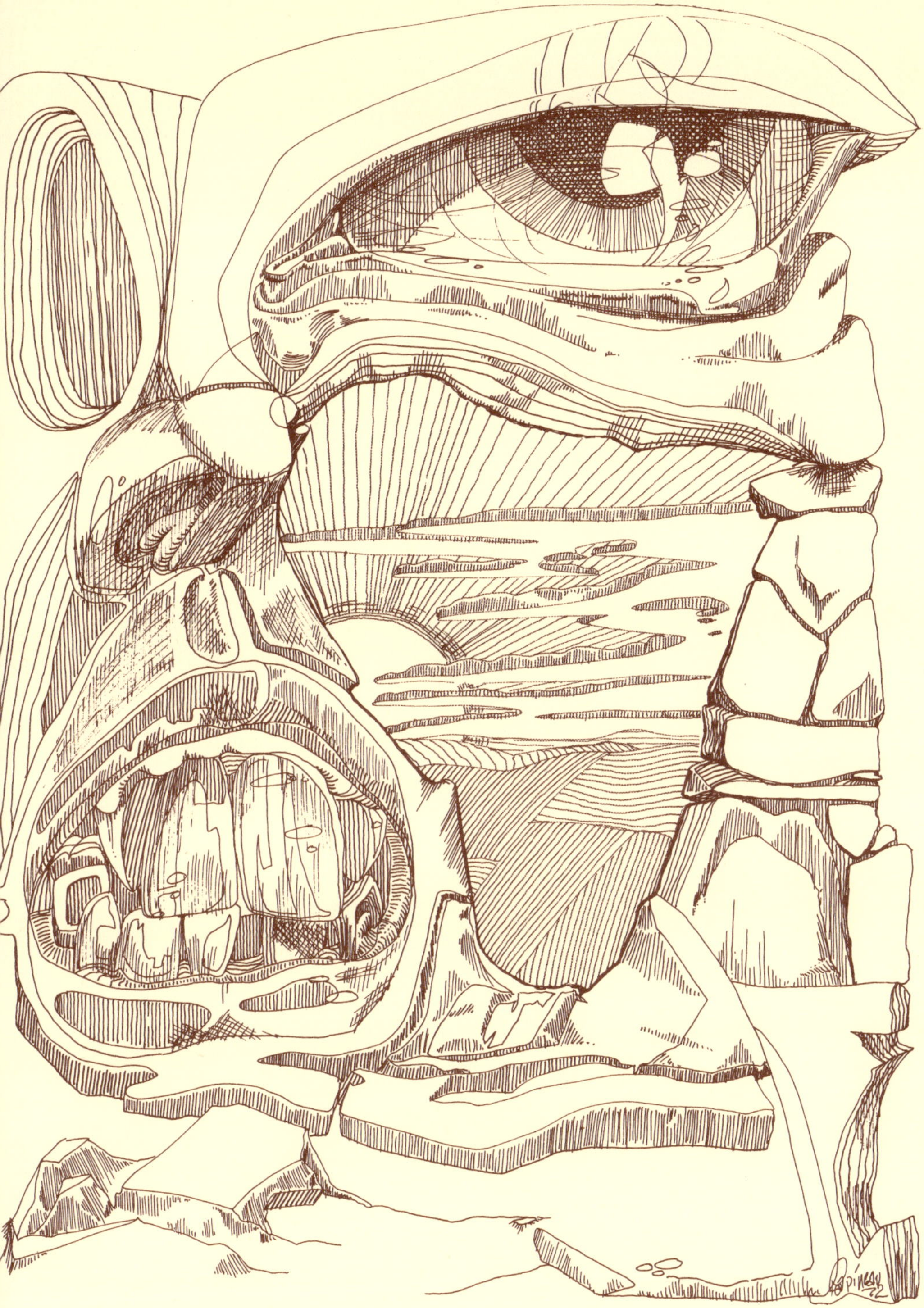

A CONTINUAL ELSEWHERE FANTASY

Since
those who remain
either
die or go astray

and

the rest
long & plan
to be
ever living —

some take suicide

to stay the
travail

(tho' not
necessarily
the Self
enduring it)

A

conquering victim
retains the posture

until that
becomes

permanent

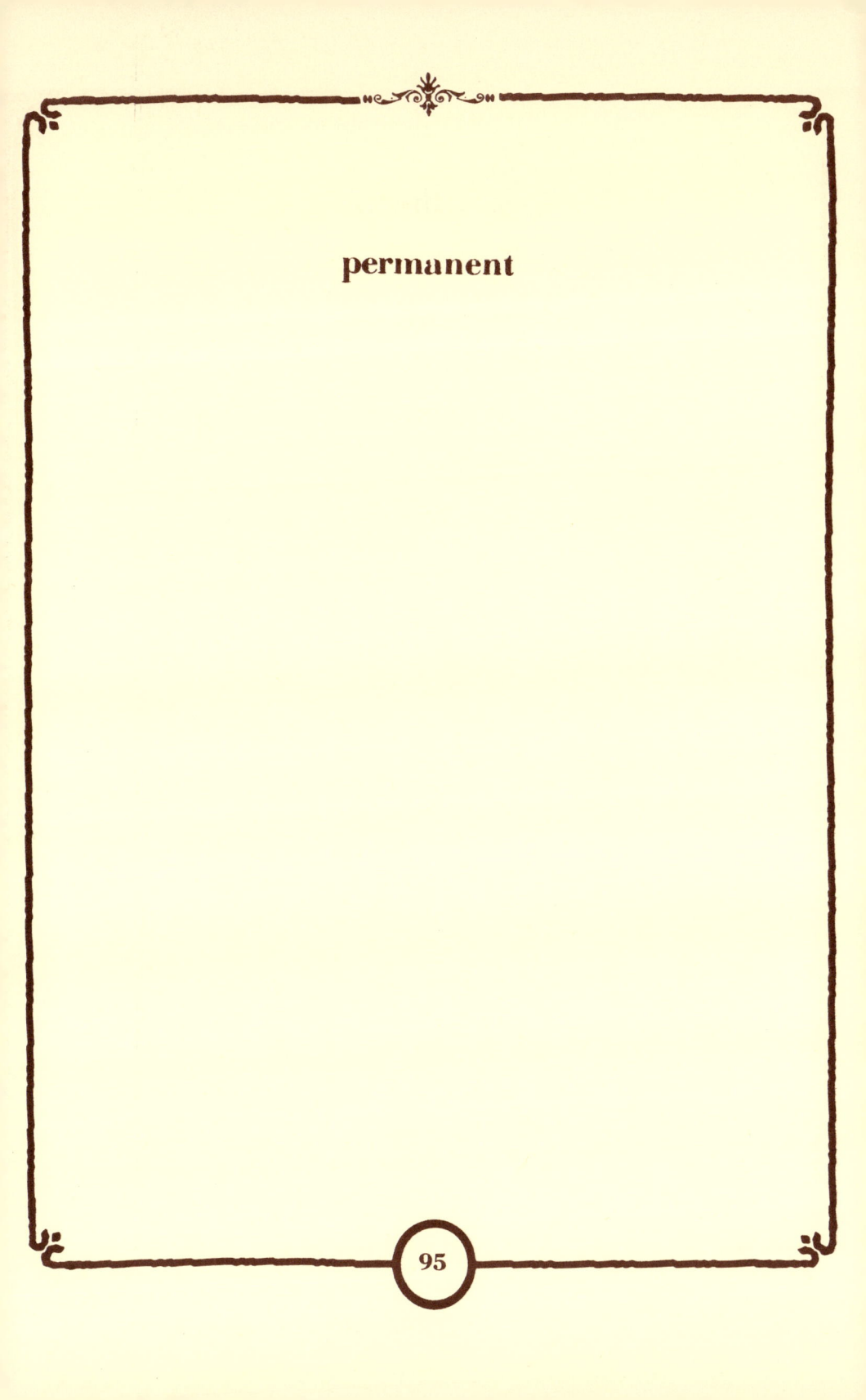

✳ MIRAGE ✳

imprint & stain

trace
on
windows
of my
Mind

proof

of my
Knows

against
those
panes

Life

brings some

exciting adventure

with
now & then
an

Oasis
of
boredom

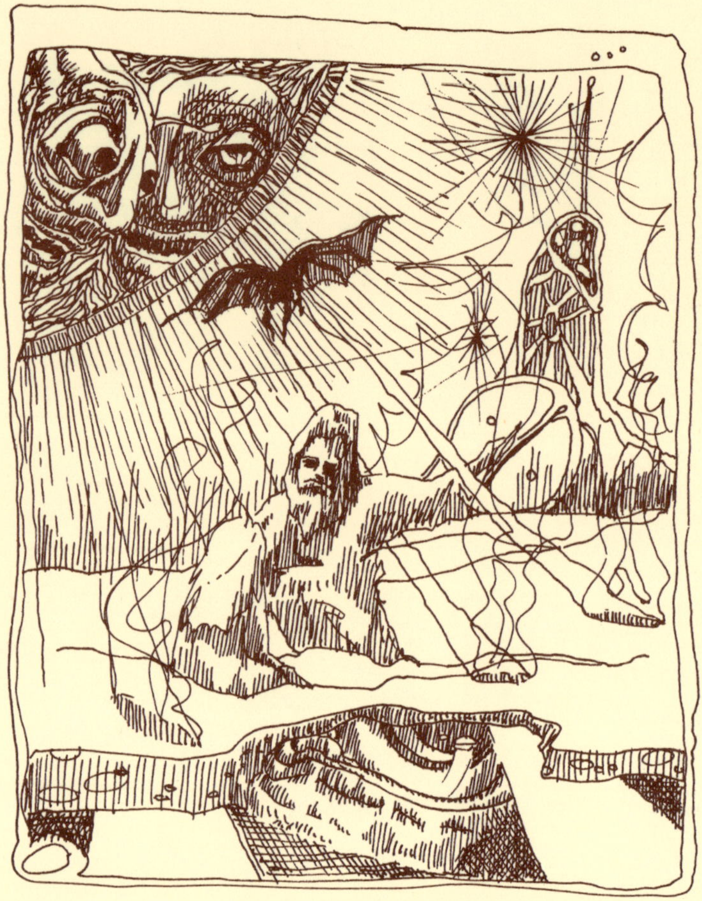

AFTERWORD

No one'll
know
the

Pleasure

I've
been

— right or wrong —

they're
dropping all around

like
flies in the brew

telling me
of the
fun

they've seen

[aye]

after a pitcher is drawn

I'm glad I'm
there

to

hear

too

EPILOGUE

Lost

— in Eden —

blindly searching

**for
the
way out**

finding

at

last

I'll

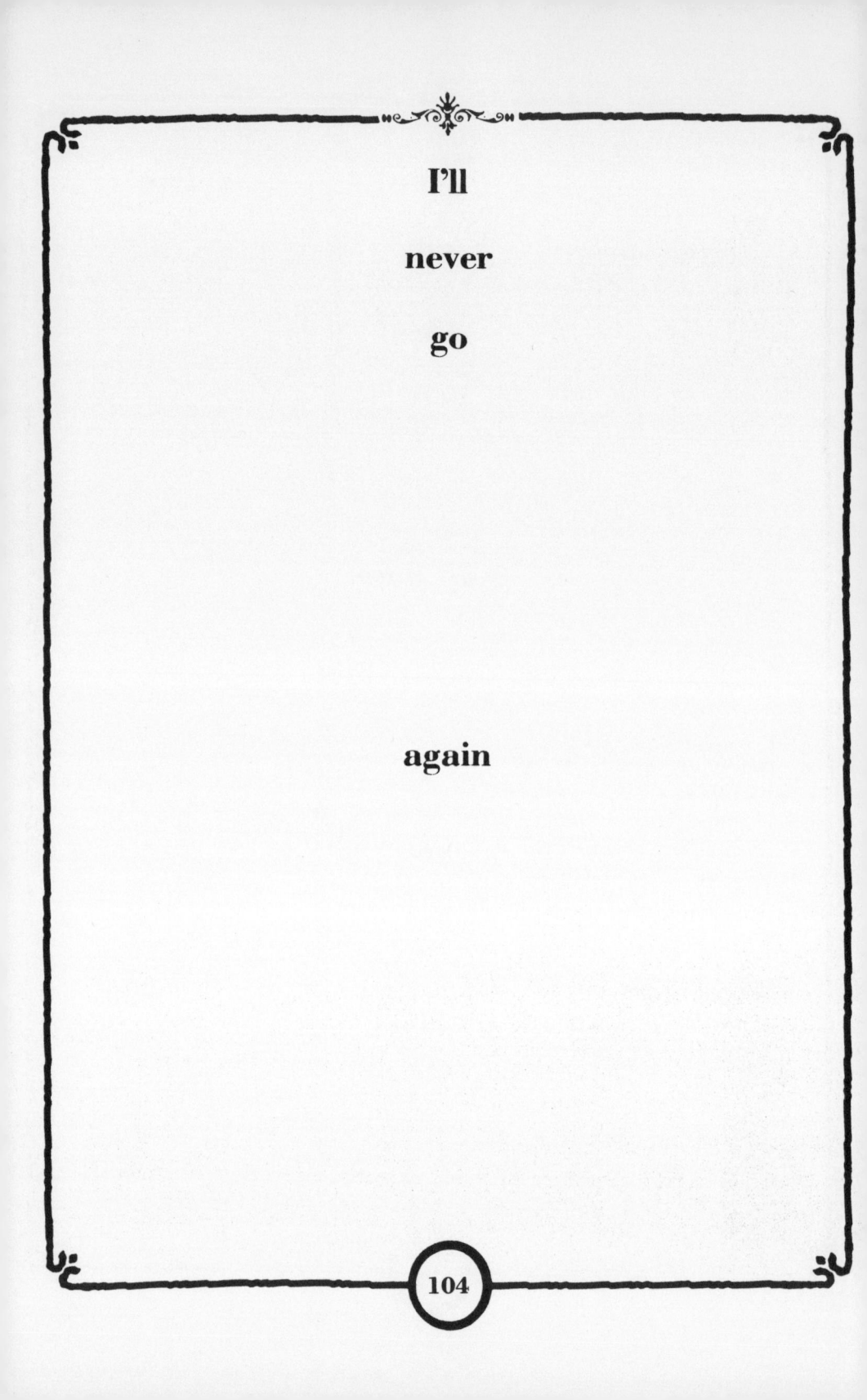

never

go

again

even

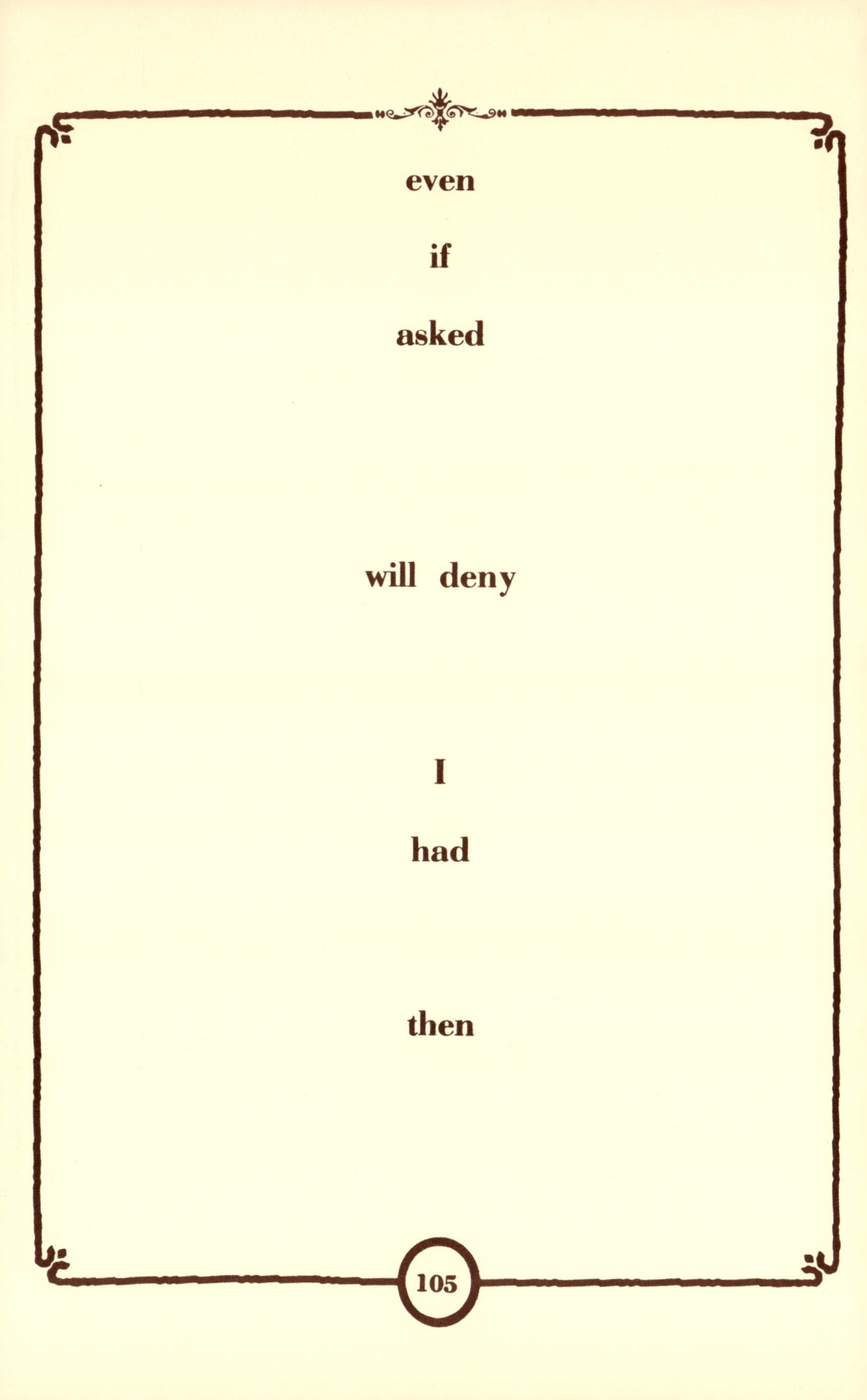

if

asked

will deny

I

had

then

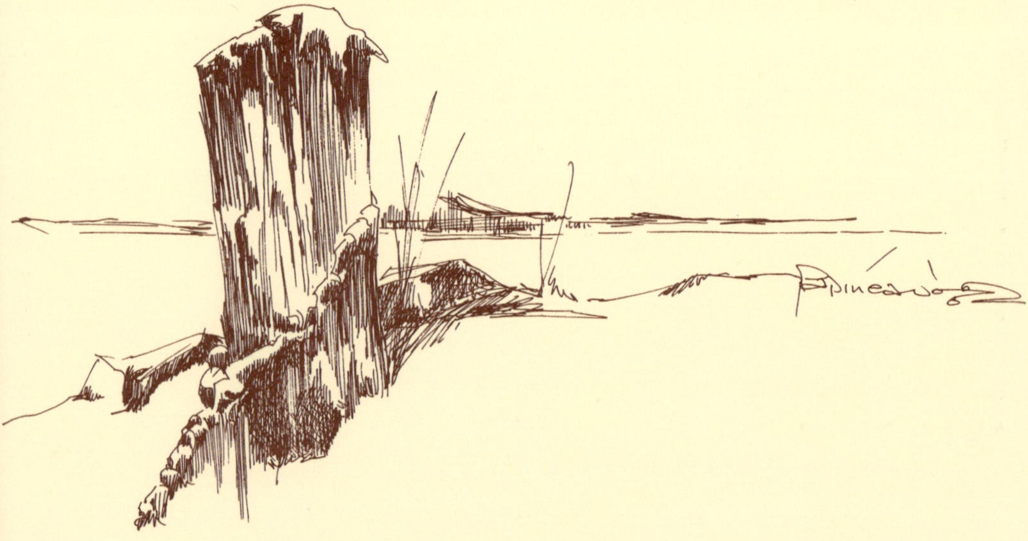

MICHAEL RAWLEY

began creative painting and writing by the early 60's while living in Los Angeles, California.

In 1973, residing in Michigan, the artist published --in a limited edition of 100 hardbound books-- handwritten selections of his 'ode and rhyme' including remarkable pen and ink illustrations from an associate artist; Papineau.

The author further developed the original manuscript and caligraphy and even the printshop skills necessary to completely produce his own book.

During 1982 Rawley presented a new hardbound, hand-lettered and rewritten *book* in a limited edition of 500.

1985 --his work having withstood the test of time is offered to the general public in its basic format with the caligraphy replaced by typesetting.

PAPINEAU

Artist, musician, poet. Papineau created the illustrations during the summer of 1972 in Michigan (where he was born).

BOOK

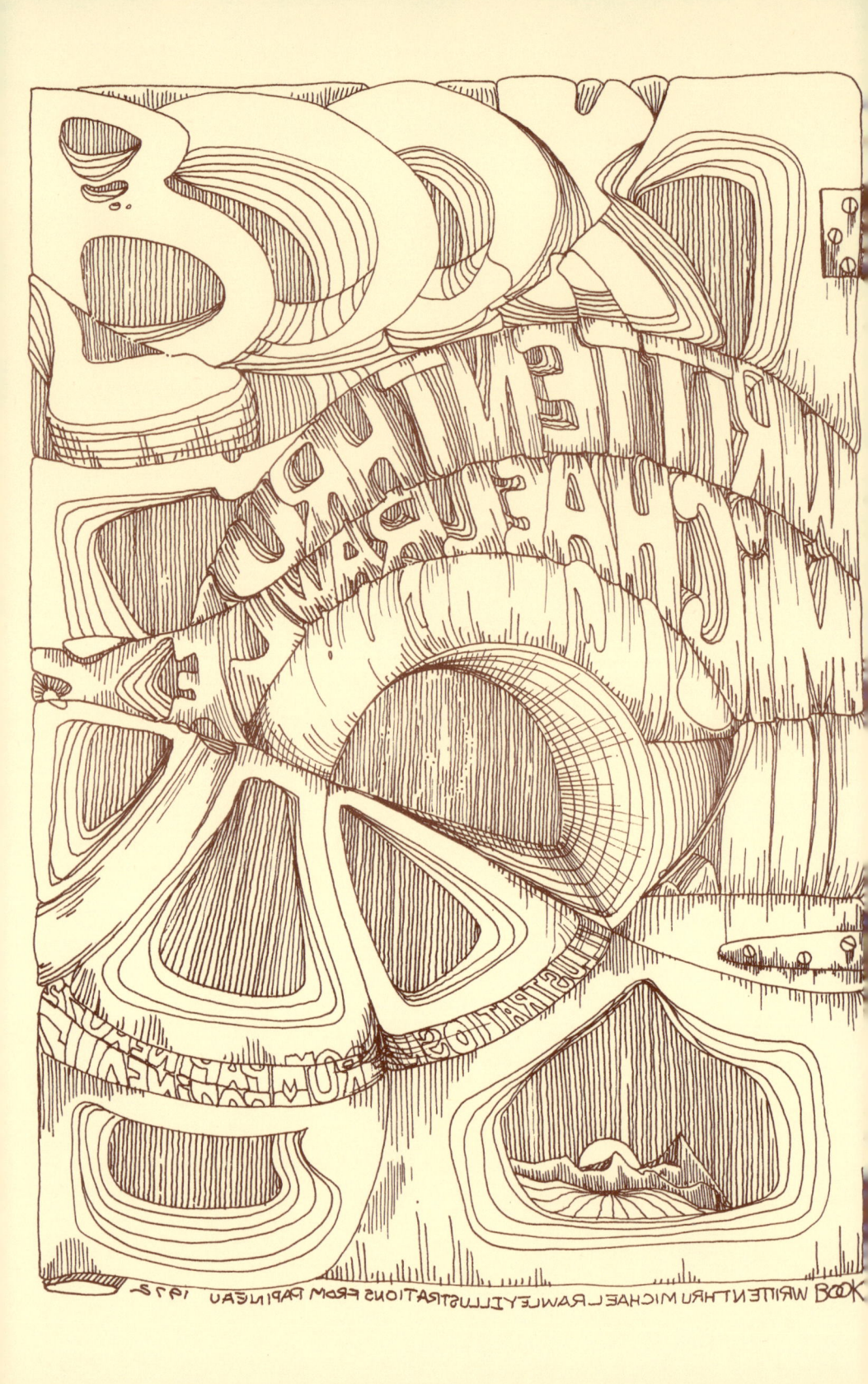

WRITTEN THRU MICHAEL RAWLEY
ILLUSTRATIONS FROM PAPINEAU
1972